THE STAIRWAY OF
a day book of wonder
SURPRSE

Betsy Pearson

Sunwarmed Sage Press | *Sheridan, Wyoming*

THE STAIRWAY OF SURPRISE: A DAY BOOK OF WONDER
COPYRIGHT © BETSY PEARSON, 2020
ALL RIGHTS RESERVED

DESIGN INTERPRETATION:
Jenae Neeson, Mybonnie Studios, Sheridan, Wyoming
mybonniestudios.com

PUBLISHED BY SUNWARMED SAGE PRESS
650 SOUTH JEFFERSON STREET
SHERIDAN, WYOMING 82801
SUNWARMEDSAGEPRESS.COM

Ordering information:
Please visit sunwarmedsagepress.com/ordering
or email sunwarmedsagepress@gmail.com

ISBN: 978-0-578-62477-8

*For Kimberly Gee
and Renée Ballard:
I didn't see you guys coming,
and now I can't imagine
the fabric of life without
our thread.*

"Pass in, pass in," the angels say, "In to the upper doors, nor count compartments of the floors, but mount to paradise by the stairway of surprise."

RALPH WALDO EMERSON

THE STAIRWAY OF SURPRISE: A DAY BOOK OF WONDER

contents

Letter to the reader

1. *Regarding Surprise*
   DAY 1 TO DAY 52

2. *Enjoying Surprise*
   DAY 53 TO DAY 148

3. *Recognizing Surprise*
   DAY 149 TO DAY 172

4. *Inviting Surprise*
   DAY 173 TO DAY 328

5. *Considering Surprise*
   DAY 329 TO DAY 356

6. *Spiriting Surprise*
   DAY 357 TO DAY 365

Dear Reader, **EACH OF THE FOLLOWING PAGES HAS SPACE FOR YOU TO RECORD THE UNEXPECTED. MY EXPERIENCE IS THAT WHEN I MAKE AN EFFORT TO NOTE THE SURPRISES OF DAILY LIFE, I NOTICE THEM MORE OFTEN, APPRECIATE THEM MORE UNIQUELY, AND FEEL LIFE A BIT MORE VITALLY.** ALTHOUGH THERE ARE PAGES ENOUGH FOR ONE YEAR OF DAILY ENTRIES, FREE YOURSELF TO USE THE PAGES IN WHATEVER WAY EVOLVES—AND PLEASE WRITE ALL OVER THEM. SURPRISE YOURSELF! *Betsy*

REGARDING SURPRISE: SAVOR AT LEAST ONE EVERY DAY.

AN UNEXPECTED FEELING OF DELIGHT, COMPLETE WITH PALPABLE SENSATIONS OF RELAXATION AND JOY. THIS PHYSICAL RELEASE IS AVAILABLE TO YOU AS A SOURCE OF HEALTH, WHOLESOMENESS, & OPTIMISM. PAY ATTENTION TO IT, AND YOUR LIFE GROWS EVER RICHER.

DAY 1

DAY 2

"Surprise is the greatest gift which life can grant us."

BORIS PASTERNAK

DAY 3

DAY 4

DAY 5

DAY 6

DAY 7

DAY 8

DAY 9

DAY 10

SURPRISED BY SURPRISE

At first you may expect very little in the way of the unexpected, yet when you begin attending to daily oddities, you may have trouble limiting your notes to the space provided here.

DAY 11

DAY 12

It's a specific kind of
GRATITUDE PRACTICE.
You find yourself thankful to be amazed so often.

DAY 13

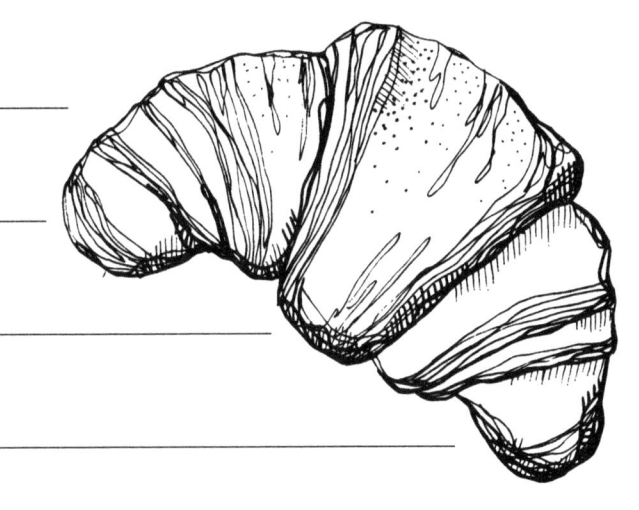

DAY 14
DAY 15

"WHERE WILL I BE FIVE YEARS FROM NOW? I DELIGHT IN NOT KNOWING. THAT'S ONE OF THE GREATEST THINGS ABOUT LIFE ITS WONDERFUL SURPRISES." —Gisele Bündchen

DAY 16

~~NOT~~ *Surprised...* **The opposite of expecting surprise is imagining that you know it all,** that you can predict what will happen. As we leave childhood, we begin to suspect that we know what each day will bring, what other people will say, and how they will act. We believe we know what to expect from this particular **season**, **hour**, **moment**.

We invest a lot of effort in trying to know what to expect. We may watch weather predictions, read our horoscopes, strive to be prepared.

DAY 17

DAY 18

DAY 19

"*A Scout is never taken by surprise...*"
SIR ROBERT BADEN-POWELL

...not ever?

DAY 20

It seemed like a good idea at the time... For cave-people, surprises could be dangerous. Those who learned to predict events and be ready for them were more successful in staying alive, finding prehistoric spouses, and producing cave-babies! But at some point, perpetual pursuit of safety merely cultivates boredom. And boredom may be the very opposite of surprise.

DAY 21

DAY 22

"THE LIFE OF THE CREATIVE MAN IS LEAD, DIRECTED AND CONTROLLED BY BOREDOM. AVOIDING BOREDOM IS ONE OF OUR MOST IMPORTANT PURPOSES." *Saul Steinber*

DAY 23

DAY 24

DAY 25

CULTIVATE INTEREST *Avoiding boredom doesn't mean you must ignore the weatherman and step into an impending storm without boots. Simply notice sights you have never seen before, facts or skills you've never learned before, and most of all people... people saying things you never could've expected, doing things you've never even heard of.*

DAY 26

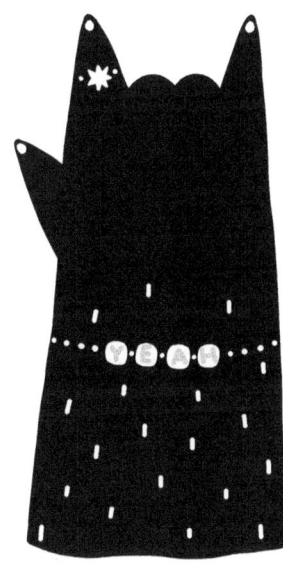

"She refused to be bored chiefly because she wasn't boring."

ZELDA FITZGERALD

DAY 27

DAY 28

EMBODYING WHAT'S NEW!

Pretty soon you're feeling life more tangibly. You feel, definitively, that each second is new, that you've never seen the sun rise on this exact day before. Not ever, in your entire life. And this realization resonates throughout your body.

DAY 29

DAY 30

DAY 31

"*Truly unexpected tidings make both ears tingle.*"

ST. BASIL

DAY 32

practice

Get in the habit of acknowledging *"never-before"* experiences. In other words, practice inexperience. You may have been taught that inexperience is not something to be proud of, much less to advertise; therefore you will need to practice a lot. Rehearse. Say it out loud:

> *I didn't know that.*
> *I've never seen that in my whole life.*
> *I've never even heard of that before!*
> *How marvelous.*

For this is what you are living–a marvel.

DAY 33

DAY 34

... AND KEEP
TRACK. WRITE IT DOWN.
AT FIRST EMPHASIZE
YOUR SENSES:
A NEW WONDER YOU'VE
NEVER SET EYES ON,
LISTENED TO,
FELT,
TASTED,
OR SMELLED.

DAY 35
WONDERS OF WONDERS

The first definition of WONDER *is as a verb:* TO THINK CURIOUSLY. *But add a few suffixes and lovely adjectives emerge: wonderful, wondrous. As you are discovering, thoughtful curiosity does indeed fill you with wonder, amazement, and astonishment.*

DAY 37

AND SO YOU MUST WONDER…

… WHERE DOES THIS CURIOSITY COME FROM? IN PART, FROM ASSUMING YOU DON'T KNOW EVERYTHING. ACTIVELY ALLOW YOURSELF THE CHANCE TO BE ASTONISHED.

DAY 38

DAY 39

DAY 40
Thunderstruck

Astonish stems from the Latin attonare: *to be struck by lightning. It makes literal sense that this same root-word morphed into stunned (astonien) and also gave us astound. All of these words capture the physicality of surprise. Attending to the unexpected is not a remote, cerebral exercise. It is visceral.*

DAY 41

DAY 42

DAY 43

*It takes your
breath away.*

*Surprise comes from prehensere:
to take or seize. Our expression*
"taken by surprise"
is exactly accurate.

DAY 44

DAY 45

DAY 46

"The moments of happiness we enjoy take us by surprise. It is not that we seize them, but that they seize us."

ASHLEY MONTAGU

Vulnerability

Perhaps, then, an obstacle to being surprised is being so protected that nothing can seize you. Boredom can't grab you, but neither will it ever transport you to new realms.

DAY 48

DAY 49
DAY 50

DAY 51

DAY 52

ENJOYING SURPRISE

Some benefits of being surprised: it feels good. After weeks of recording the unexpected, you are probably experiencing how, above all, surprise feels strangely agreeable – a sensation more intense than regular pleasure. It is delight-full, or as lewis thomas put it, a "contented dazzlement."

DAY 53 DAY 54

> "Everything that is new or uncommon raises a pleasure in the imagination, because it fills the soul with an agreeable surprise, gratifies its curiosity, and gives it an idea of which it was not before possessed."
>
> **JOSEPH ADDISON**

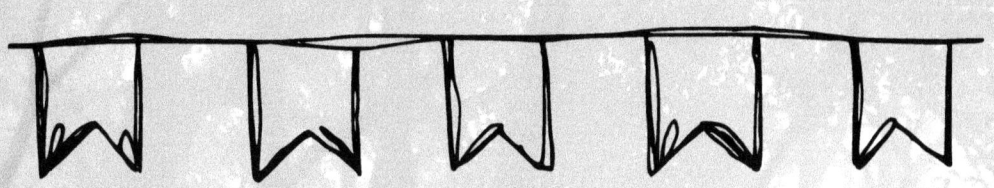

DAY 55
DAY 56

DAY 57

DAY 58

"THE BIGGEST BORE IS THE PERSON WHO IS BORED BY EVERYONE AND EVERYTHING." FRANK TYGER

*It's no surprise that
all kinds of relationships thrive.
When you're paying attention, waiting
to see if another will say or do anything
unusual, you are, by definition, interested.*

DAY 59

DAY 60

DAY 61

DAY 62

DAY 63

DAY 64

DAY 65

YOUR INTEREST

DAY 66

DAY 67

GENERATES
energy

This recognition of the unexpected energizes us to connect with others...

DAY 68

... and in those others, we find an even deeper source of the unexpected.

DAY 69

DAY 70

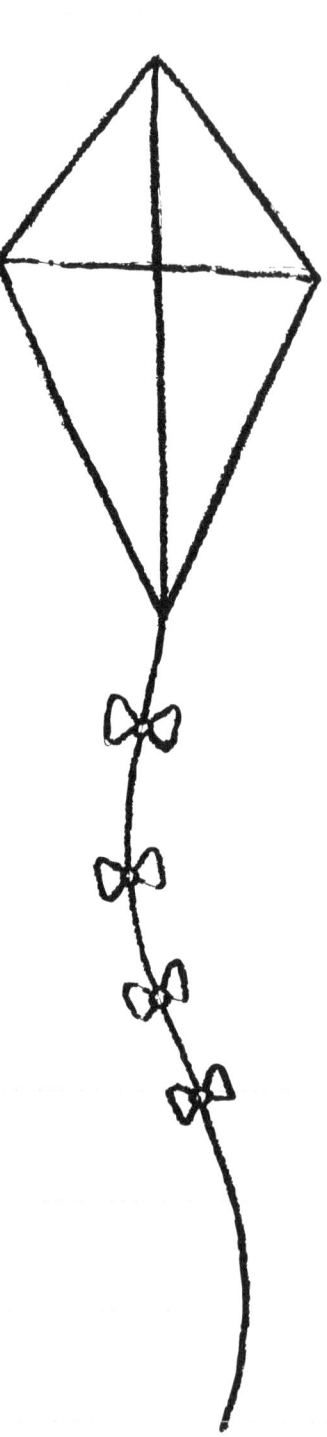

DAY 71 | **DAY 72**

"NONE OF US KNOW ALL THE POTENTIALITIES THAT SLUMBER IN THE SPIRIT OF THE POPULATION, OR ALL THE WAYS IN WHICH THAT POPULATION CAN SURPRISE US WHEN THERE IS THE RIGHT INTERPLAY OF EVENTS."

VÁCLAV HAVEL

DAY 74

Engaging more curiously with the world around us is likely to have one especially unexpected effect...

"I MET A LOT OF PEOPLE IN EUROPE. I EVEN ENCOUNTERED MYSELF."

James Baldwin

DAY 75
DAY 76

DAY 77

DAY 78

DAY 79

"It's a great thing when you realize you still have the ability to surprise yourself. Makes you wonder what else you can do that you've forgotten about." Alan Ball, American Beauty

With the possibility of the unknown, there is possibility for movement even in the knotty, stuck areas of a life.

DAY 80

DAY 81

BAD HABITS HATE SURPRISE!

WHEN WE SEE LIFE'S SURPRISES, WE ARE LESS LIKELY TO SEEK UNHEALTHY WAYS OF DUCKING THE DULL.

DAY 82

DAY 83

DAY 84

DAY 85
DAY 86

"Boredom is a vital problem for the moralist, since at least half the sins of mankind are caused by the fear of it." Bertrand Russell

DAY 87

"PROCRASTINATION AVOIDS BOREDOM; ONE NEVER HAS THE FEELING THAT THERE IS NOTHING TO DO."

A Law attributed to Murphy

DAY 88

DAY 89

DAY 90

DAY 91

"UNCERTAINTY & MYSTERY ARE ENERGIES OF LIFE. DON'T LET THEM SCARE YOU UNDULY, FOR THEY KEEP BOREDOM AT BAY AND SPARK CREATIVITY."

R. I. Fitzhenry

DAY 92

WAIT, IT'S ART?!

DAY 93
DAY 94

As you set about uncovering the unknown, you find yourself inventing opportunities for discovery, and crafting new experiences. Suddenly you are deep in the creative process.

DAY 95
DAY 96

DAY 97

"Mystery is at the heart of creativity. That, and surprise."

Julia Cameron

DAY 98

DAY 99

"Art must take reality by surprise."

F. Sagan

DAY 100

DAY 101

DAY 102

Courting amazement, you fall into innovation

You will discover fundamentally new ways of approaching issues and solving problems, whether they are dilemmas of design, housekeeping, relationship, career, or spirit.

"If it's surprising, it's useful." Tom Hirshfield
DAY 103

DAY 104

DAY 105

EVEN BETTER THAN ETHICS, ART, OR INNOVATION: LAUGHTER!

DAY 106

DAY 107

> "A laugh is a surprise."
> — CHEVY CHASE

DAY 108

DAY 109

You might just find yourself funnier too.

DAY 110

"THE SECRET TO HUMOR IS SURPRISE."

DAY 111 ARISTOTLE

DAY 112

DAY 113

"SURPRISE ME."

Yogi Berra (to his wife's question: "If you go before I do, where would you like me to have you buried?")

it's good

DAY 114

DAY 115

for you!

LAUGHING, ESPECIALLY AT THE POTENTIALLY UNPLEASANT PARTS OF LIFE, BENEFITS HEALTH. STALKING SURPRISE MAY VERY WELL BE CRUCIAL TO YOUR WELL BEING. IF YOU THINK ABOUT IT, SOME MEASURE OF SURPRISE IS UNAVOIDABLE, SO WHY NOT EMBRACE—RATHER THAN FEAR—IT?

DAY 116

DAY 117
DAY 118

DAY 119

"Grasp your opportunities, no matter how poor your health; nothing is worse for your health than boredom." — MIGNON MCLAUGHLIN, THE SECOND NEUROTIC'S NOTEBOOK

DAY 120

DAY 121

A DIFFERENT PERSPECTIVE

The pleasure, connections, self-discovery, art, movement, humor, and healthiness of surprise may come from its instant change in how we look at one thing... and therefore everything.

DAY 122

DAY 123
DAY 124

DAY 125

"PERHAPS THE TRUTH DEPENDS ON A WALK AROUND THE LAKE."
Wallace Stevens

DAY 126

DAY 127 | DAY 128

"TO BE SURPRISED, TO WONDER, IS TO BEGIN TO UNDERSTAND."

José Ortega y Gasset

DAY 129

"WONDER IS THE BEGINNING OF WISDOM"... GREEK PROVERB

DAY 130

DAY 131
DAY 132

DAY 133

DAY 134

"WONDER RATHER THAN DOUBT IS THE ROOT OF KNOWLEDGE"
Abraham Joshua Heschel

DAY 135

DAY 136

DAY 137

If the Unknown is NOT-SCARY...

... if the "unheard of" is now a source of delight, then facing life (AND BEYOND) is much less frightening.

DAY 138

DAY 139

"Life is a great surprise. I don't see why death should not be an even greater one." Vladimir Nabokov

DAY 140

DAY 141

Trying to avoid surprise by thorough preparation is strenuous. Trying to plan elaborate ways of being entertained is tiresome.

Both can be costly.

Enjoying the surprises life springs upon you brings a sweet happiness... with much less work.

DAY 142

DAY 143

"EXPECT NOTHING. LIVE FRUGALLY ON SURPRISE."

DAY 144

DAY 145

surprise:
is this love?

DAY 146

DAY 147   DAY 148

"Love withers with predictability; its very essence is surprise and amazement. To make love a prisoner of the mundane is to take its passion and lose it forever."

LEO BUSCAGLIA

Recognizing Surprise

SURPRISE ISN'T ALWAYS OBVIOUS. CHERISH THE UNEXPECTED IN ITS SUBTLE FORMS.

DAY 151

"STATISTICALLY, THE PROBABILITY OF ANY OF US BEING HERE IS SO SMALL THAT YOU'D THINK THE MERE FACT OF EXISTING WOULD KEEP US ALL IN CONTENTED DAZZLEMENT OF SURPRISE." *Lewis Thomas*

DAY 152

DAY 153

DAY 154

IT CAN BE LEARNING SOMETHING YOU DIDN'T KNOW.

New knowledge is always a surprise: the little facts, the huge revelation, and everything in between.

DAY 155

It definitely includes learning about that thing you never knew you didn't know...

DAY 156

DAY 157

... AND SENSING THE DELICACIES OF EACH SENSE.

Even slight changes in smell, taste, sound, and feel are surprising—never mind each new place, person, book, art, music, phrase, and word choice you encounter as you move through your day

DAY 158

DAY 159

A New Wondering

DAY 160

DAY 161

OBSERVE PEOPLE.

EAVESDROP ON STRANGERS, MEET NEW FOLKS, OR SEEK OUT YOUR MOST UNCONVENTIONAL ACQUAINTANCES. THEN GRADUATE INTO STUDYING THE PEOPLE YOU THINK ARE MOST PREDICTABLE. EVEN YOURSELF.

DAY 162

DAY 163

WRITE OUT-OF-CHARACTER
PERFORMANCES BY
SOMETHING YOU THOUGHT
WAS COMPLETELY UNKNOWN

DAY 164

DAY 165

DAY 166

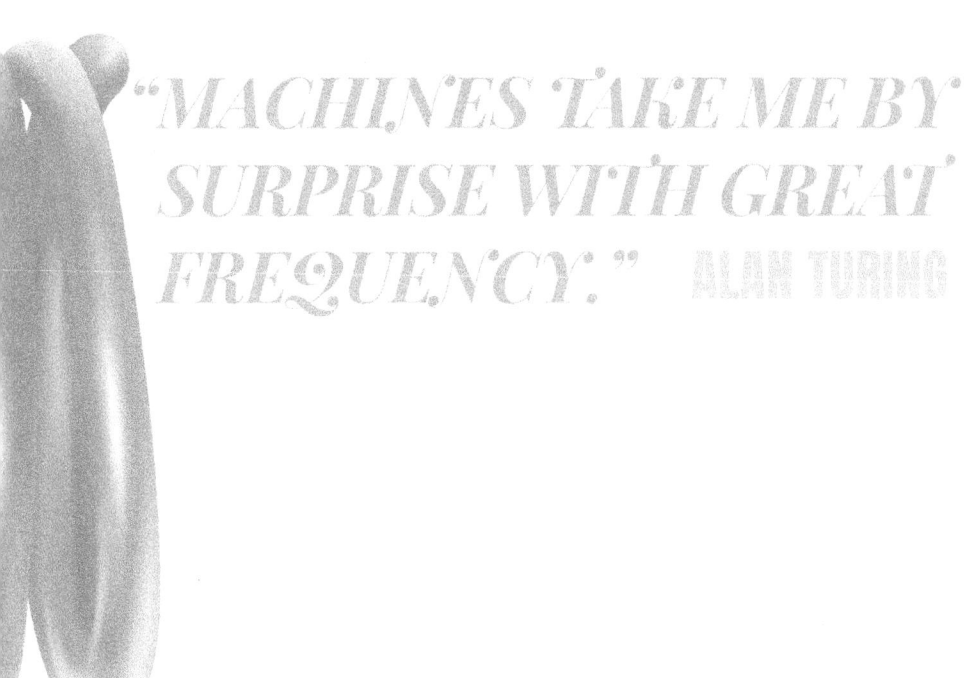

"MACHINES TAKE ME BY SURPRISE WITH GREAT FREQUENCY." —ALAN TURING

DAY 167

But don't minimize the old, obvious, impossible-to-ignore symptoms of surprise:

TEARS

A GRIN

LAUGHTER

HAIR STANDING UP ON THE TOP OF YOUR HEAD
(or all over your body!)

Or the masquerading tricks of the mind...

IS ANGER SOMETIMES A SIGN OF SURPRISE?

CONFUSION??

DUMBFOUNDED-NESS!

DAY 168

DAY 170

DAY 171

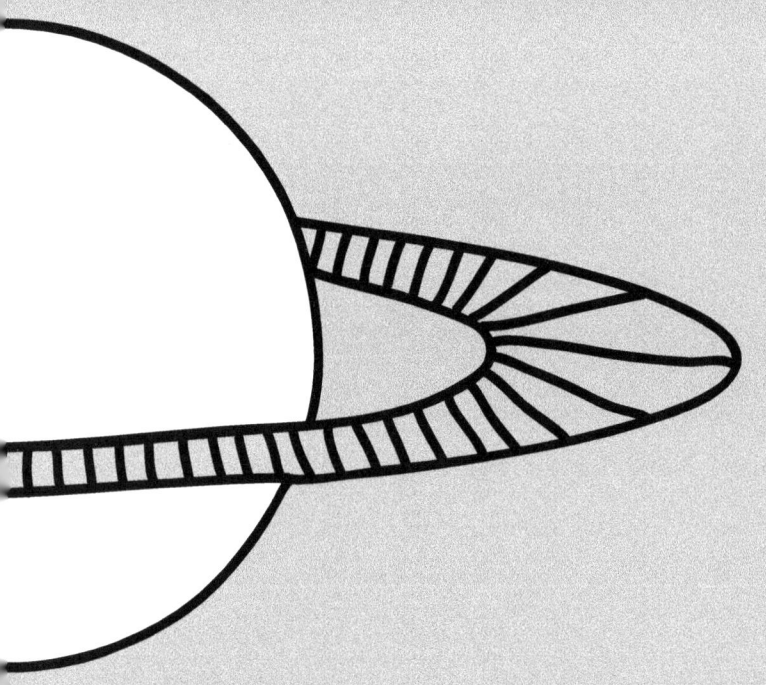

DAY 172

INVITING
SURPRISE

RECORD IT & IT SHALL COME

Expecting there will be

something unexpected

to write down

encourages surprise

in your life.

DAY 173

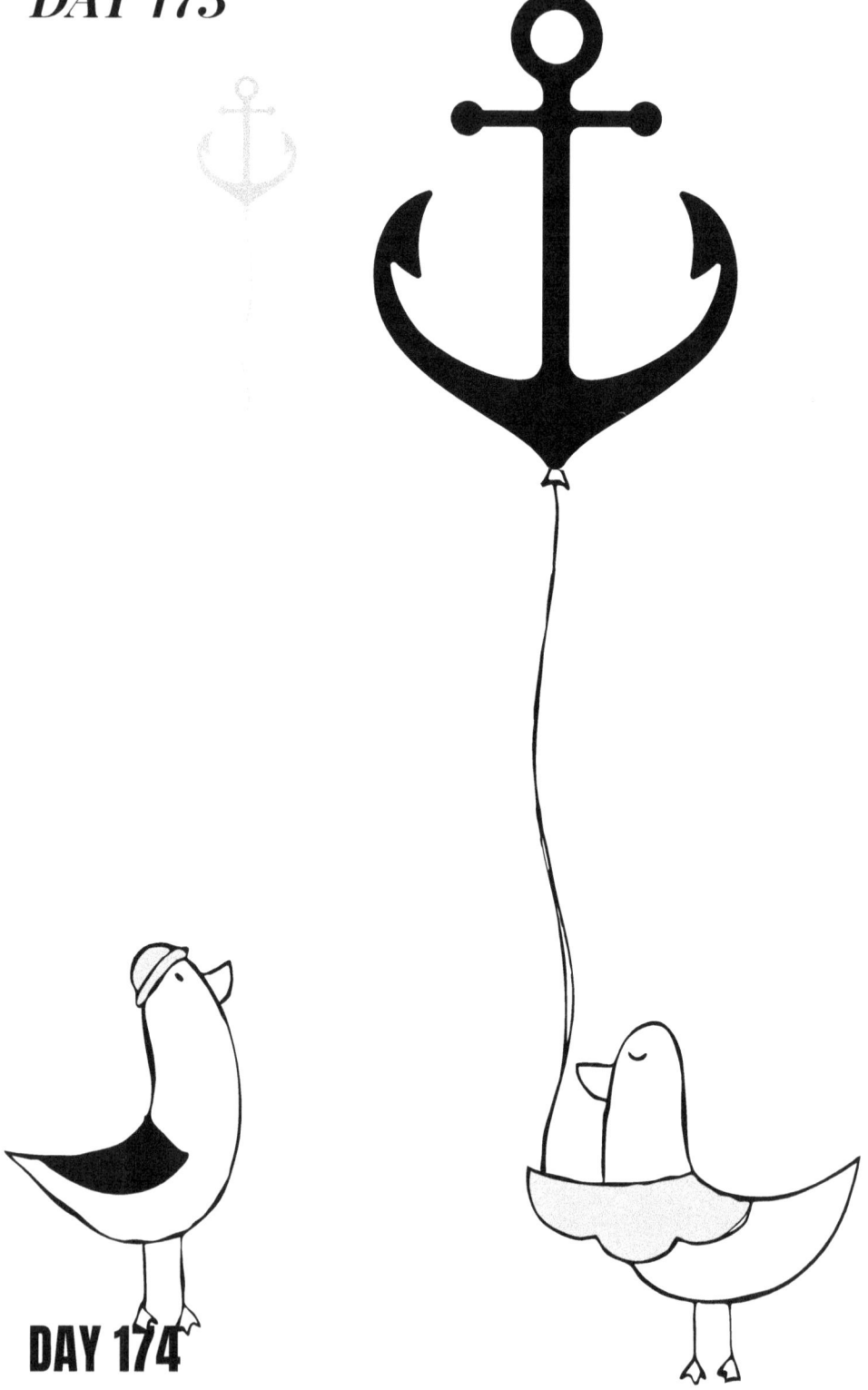

DAY 174

DAY 175
DAY 176

"If you do not expect the unexpected, you will not find it, for it is not to be reached by search or trail."

Heraclitus

"Nobody is bored when he is trying to make something that is beautiful or to discover something that is true."
W. R. Inge

Take a class.

DAY 177
DAY 178

DAY 179

DAY 180

HELP SOMEONE OUT.

EAT ME!

DAY ONE8ONE | DAY ONE8TWO

DAY 183

"THE PLEASURE WE DERIVE FROM DOING FAVORS IS PARTLY IN THE FEELING IT GIVES US THAT WE ARE NOT ALTOGETHER WORTHLESS. IT IS A PLEASANT SURPRISE TO OURSELVES." —ERIC HOFFER

DAY 184

DAY 185
DAY 186

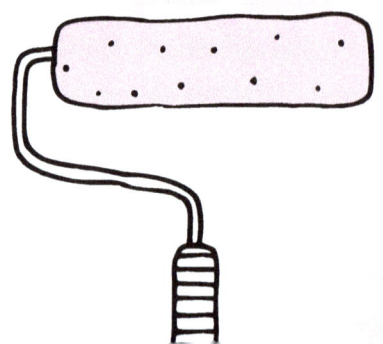

DAY 187
DAY 188

DAY 189

➢ *Openly wonder.*

DAY 190

DAY 191

>>

DAY 192

DAY 193

"*A sudden bold and unexpected question doth many times surprise a man and lay him open.*" Francis Bacon

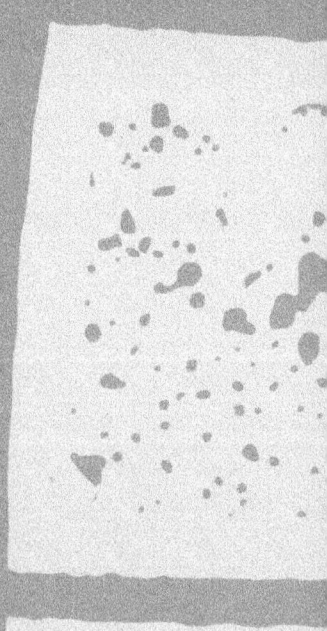

DAY 194

DAY 195
DAY 196

DAY 197

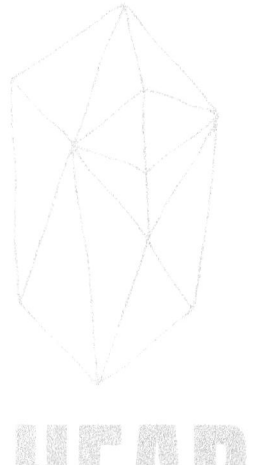

HEAR.

"The cure for boredom is curiosity. There is no cure for curiosity."
Dorothy Parker

DAY 198

DAY 199

> "*Bore, n.: A person who talks when you wish him to listen.*"
>
> Ambrose Bierce
> *The Devil's Dictionary*

DAY 2000(actually only 200):

DAY 201

look at yourself

DAY 202

DAY 203

or not...

"Do not know yourself.
I want to continue
to surprise me."

Arielle Dombasle

DAY 204

DAY 205

DAY 206

> "SOMEONE'S BORING ME. I THINK IT'S ME."
>
> — *Dylan Thomas*

DAY 207

DAY 208

DAY 209

DAY 210

Hang out in nature

light–cloud–precipitation–season–time-of-day

DAY 211 *(divider line)* **DAY 212**

*"Every spring is the only spring,
a perpetual astonishment."*

Ellis Peters

DAY 215

Don't worry about efficiency.

"Boredom is the feeling that everything is a waste of time; serenity, that nothing is."
Thomas S. Szasz

DAY 216

DAY 217

DAY 218

RELEASE REQUIREMENTS

DAY 219
DAY 220

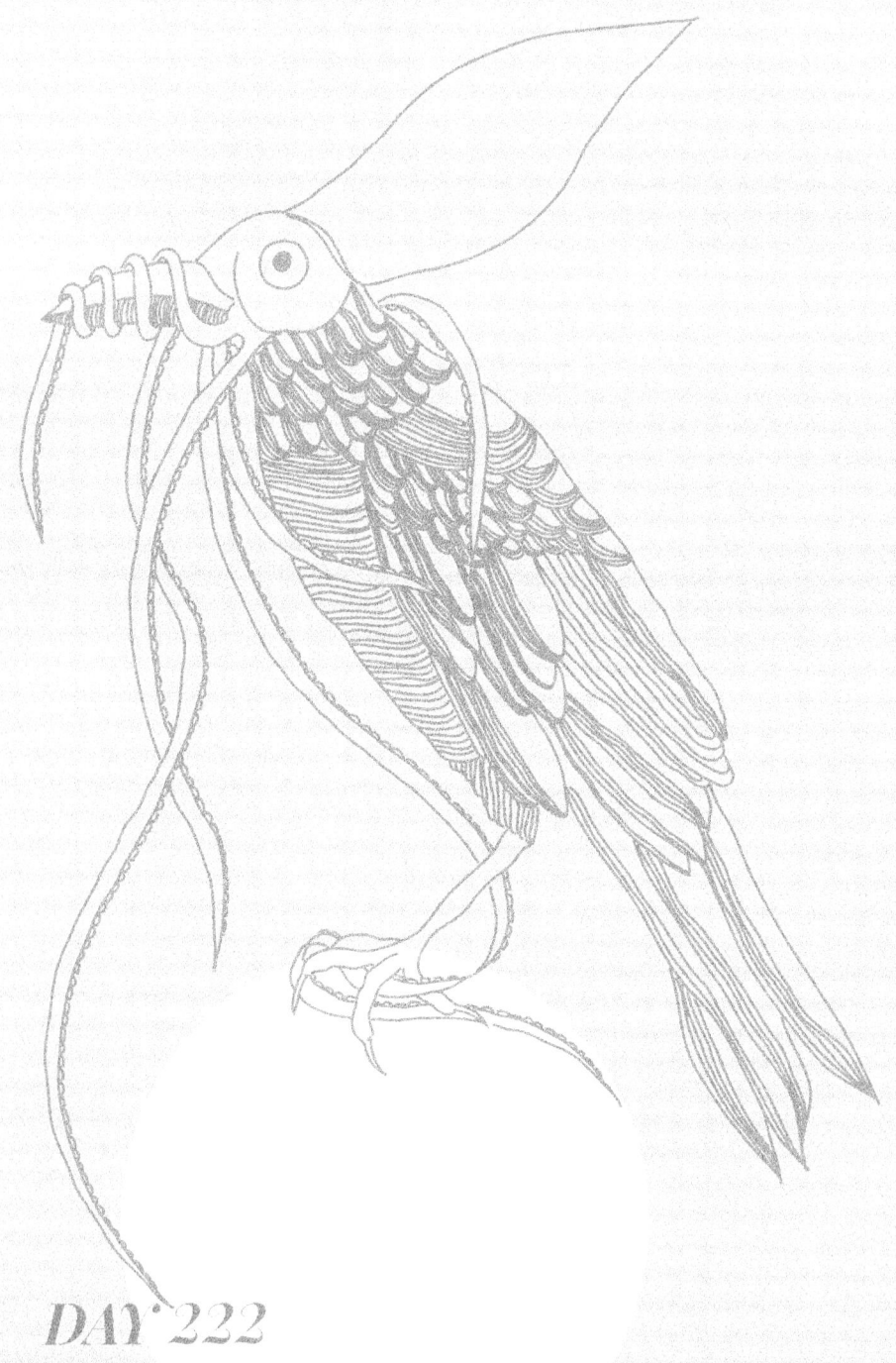

DAY 222

"THE BEST THINGS IN LIFE ARE UNEXPECTED— BECAUSE THERE WERE NO EXPECTATIONS."

Eli Khamarov

DAY 225

TRY AN ACTIVITY
COMPLETELY UNKNOWN TO YOU.

"Wonder is from surprise, and

DAY 226

DAY 227

surprise stops with "EXPERIENCE."

Bishop Robert South

DAY 228

DAY 229

"IDEALLY, I'D LIKE TO BE THE ETERNAL NOVICE, FOR THEN ONLY THE SURPRISES WOULD BE ENDLESS."
KEITH JARRETT

DAY 230

DAY 231
DAY 232
UNDERTAKE BASIC RESEARCH.

"This is the element that distinguishes applied science from basic. Surprise is what makes the difference... What you need at the outset is a high degree of uncertainty; otherwise it isn't likely to be an important problem. You start with an incomplete roster of facts, characterized by their ambiguity; often the problem consists of discovering the connections between unrelated pieces of information."
Lewis Thomas

DAY 233

DAY 234

DAY 235
DAY 236

DAY 237

> *"The way to do research is to attack the facts at the point of greatest astonishment"*
> — CELIA GREEN

DAY 238

DAY 239

> ANTHROPOLOGY DEMANDS THE OPEN-MINDEDNESS WITH WHICH ONE MUST LOOK AND LISTEN, RECORD IN ASTONISHMENT AND WONDER THAT WHICH ONE WOULD NOT HAVE BEEN ABLE TO GUESS.

Margaret Mead

DAY 240

Forsake doctrine.

"When we blindly adopt a religion, a political system, a literary dogma, we become automatons. We cease to grow."

ANAIS NIN

DAY 241   **DAY 242**

DAY 243 **DAY 244**

DAY 245

DAY 246

HIT THE OPEN ROAD.

"To my mind, the greatest reward and luxury of travel is to be able to experience everyday things as if for the first time, to be in a position in which almost nothing is so familiar it is taken for granted." BILL BRYSON

DAY 247

DAY 248

DAY 249

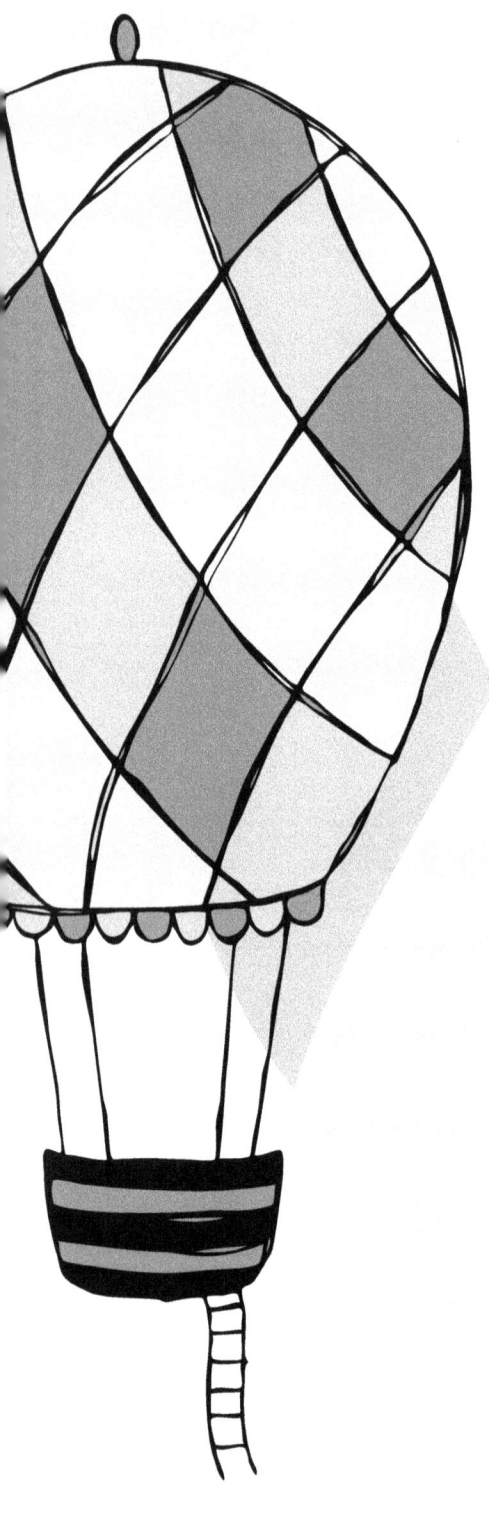

DAY 250

DAY 251

"Unexpected travel suggestions are dancing lessons from God"

Kurt Vonnegut, Jr.

DAY 252

DAY 253

MAKE A MAP

As you try to draw a place, include details, and grasp their relative relationships, you will discover unpredicted existences and exciting connections.

DAY 254

"I HAVE AN EXISTENTIAL MAP; IT HAS 'YOU ARE HERE' WRITTEN ALL OVER IT." *Stephen Wright*

DAY 255

DAY 256

DAY 257

DAY 258

DAY 259

TAKE NOTHING FOR GRANTED...
BUDDHISTS MEDITATE ON DEATH TO APPRECIATE EVERY BIT OF LIFE. THE ANCIENT ROMANS DID THE SAME.

"THINK TO YOURSELF THAT EVERY DAY IS YOUR LAST; THE HOUR TO WHICH YOU DO NOT LOOK FORWARD WILL COME AS A WELCOME SURPRISE." *HORACE*

DAY 260

DO ART,

DAY 261 | DAY 262

ANY KIND.

> "The real artist's work is a surprise to himself."
>
> *Robert Henri*

DAY 263 | DAY 264

DAY 265

DAY 266

Write.

"Whatever extra there is in me at any given moment isn't fully formed. I am hardly aware of it; it awaits the next book. It will—with luck—come to me during the actual writing, and it will take me by surprise."
—V. S. Naipaul

DAY 267 | DAY 268

DAY 269

POW POW POW

Or shoot pix. 📷

DAY 270

DAY 271

"NO PLACE IS BORING, IF YOU'VE HAD A GOOD NIGHT'S SLEEP AND HAVE A POCKET FULL OF UNEXPOSED FILM."
Robert Adams

DAY 272

DAY 273

DAY 274

SEEK QUIET.

DAY 275

DAY 276

DAY 277

"IT IS ONLY WHEN WE SILENT THE BLARING SOUNDS OF OUR DAILY EXISTENCE THAT WE CAN FINALLY HEAR THE WHISPERS OF TRUTH THAT LIFE REVEALS TO US, AS IT STANDS KNOCKING ON THE DOORSTEPS OF OUR HEARTS."
K.T. JONG

DAY 278

DAY 279

DAY 280

DAY 281

work.

"Are you bored with life? Then throw yourself into some work you believe in with all your heart, live for it, die for it, and you will find happiness that you had thought could never be yours."

DALE CARNEGIE

DAY 282

DAY 283

DAY 284

DAY 285

"**WORK SPARES US FROM THREE EVILS: BOREDOM, VICE, AND NEED.**" *Voltaire*

DAY 287

> "Everything considered, work is less boring than amusing oneself."

CHARLES BAUDELAIRE

DAY 288

DAY 289

DAY 290

DAY 291

*"Life is full of surprises.
Just say 'never' and you'll see."*
ANONYMOUS

DAY 292

DAY 293

Definitely break your routine:

DAY 294

> "Habitualization devours work, clothes, furniture, one's wife, and the fear of war." **VIKTOR SHKLOVSKY**

DAY 295

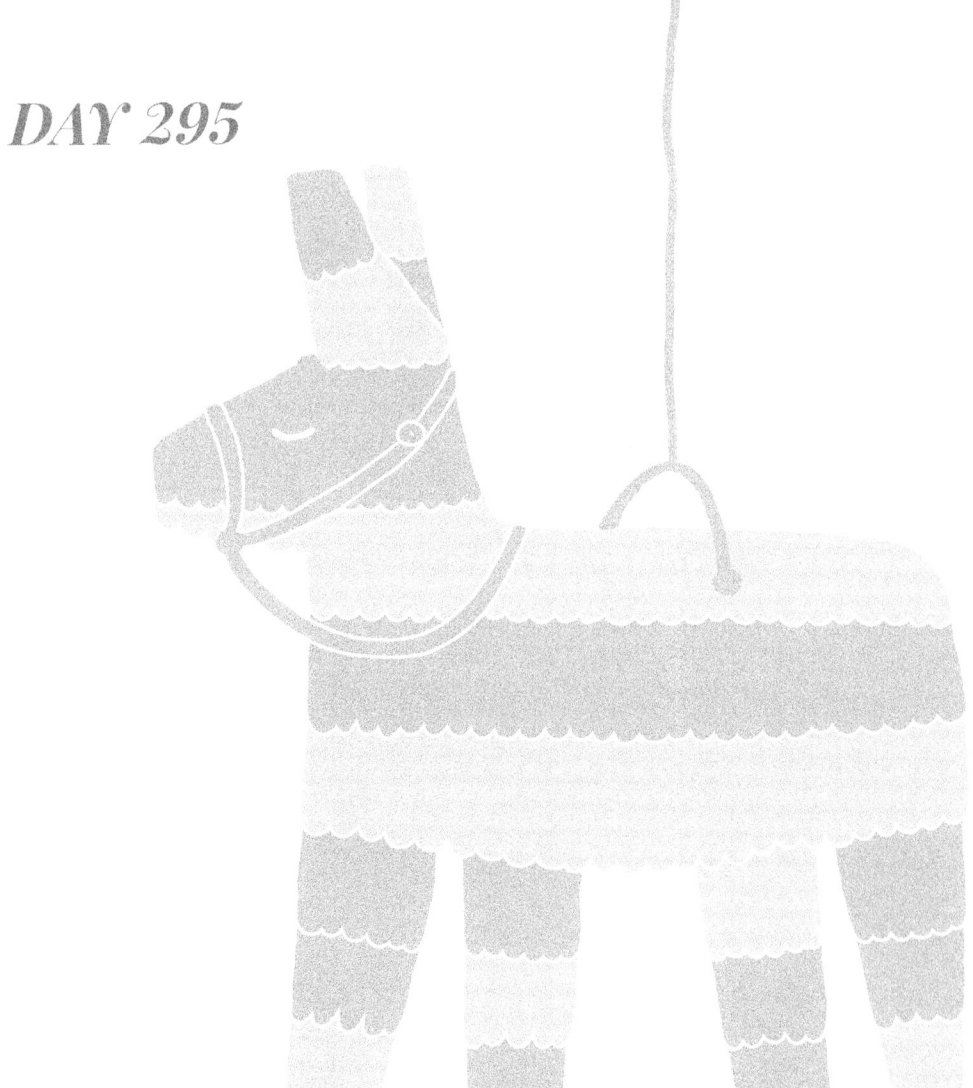

DAY 296

BREAK RULES
(you can invent them first if you want!)

DAY 298
DAY 297

DAY 299

DAY 300

"One wonders what would happen in a society in which there were no rules to break. Doubtless everyone would quickly die of boredom." Susan Howitch

DAY: 301
CONCOCT

the story
of your
day. Even
better
than a
Hollywood
conquest.

DAY: 302

DAY 303

"AND TO THINK THAT I SAW IT ON MULBERRY STREET!" —DR. SEUSS

DAY 304

LOSE THE SOPHISTICATION

"SOPHISTICATED"
shares a root word with "SOPHOMORIC"
as well as "SOPHIST"
someone trained right out of childlike wonder.

DAY 305
DAY 306

DAY 307

"ONCE THEY ARE THROUGH THE PROCESS OF EDUCATION, MOST PEOPLE LOSE THE CAPACITY OF WONDERING, OF BEING SURPRISED. THEY FEEL THEY OUGHT TO KNOW EVERYTHING, AND HENCE THAT IT IS A SIGN OF IGNORANCE TO BE SURPRISED OR PUZZLED BY ANYTHING."

Erich Fromm

DAY 308

DAY 309 / DAY 310

SURPRISE OTHERS!

"IF YOU WANT TO PUT NEW LIFE INTO YOUR BUSINESS, INTO YOUR JOB, INTO YOUR RELATIONSHIPS, THINK OF HOW YOU CAN DEPART FROM THE NORM, GO THE SECOND MILE, **OFFER YOUR TIME, AND**

PLEASANTLY SURPRISE THEM
WHEN THEY LEAST EXPECT IT.
WE ARE ALL SEARCHING FOR
SURPRISE IN LIFE." *RICHARD N. BOLLES*

DAY 311 ⋮ **DAY 312**

DAY 313

DAY 314

DAY 315

Allow someone to love

DAY 316

DAY 317

Read all kinds of things.

"If you resist reading what you disagree with, how will you ever acquire deeper insights into what you believe? The things most worth reading are precisely those that challenge our convictions." ANONYMOUS

DAY 318

DAY 319
DAY 320

ABOVE ALL, BE BRAVE.

Remember, it's not courageous if you're not afraid. Bravery doesn't mean the fear goes away, just that you "feel the fear and do it anyway" (as Susan Jeffers titled her classic book).

DAY 322

"In order to live free and happily, you must sacrifice boredom. It is not always an easy sacrifice." —Richard Bach

DAY 323
DAY 324

DAY 325

give thanks

It is true that a Surprise Journal is one form of gratitude practice. And, in turn, dwelling each day on one thing for which you're thankful will lead you to surprises.

DAY 326

DAY 327

DAY 328

CONSIDERING SURPRISE

What's really happening when we are flabbergasted?

DAY 329
DAY 330

DAY 332

DAY 331

a shift

ECSTASY ORIGINALLY CAME FROM THE GREEK FOR "NOT IN STASIS" AND MEANT "DISPLACEMENT." OUR MODERN MEANING IS RAPTUROUS DELIGHT. AH! RAPTURE, FROM THE LATIN WORD FOR SEIZED, TRANSPORTS US WITH EMOTION, CARRIES US OFF SPIRITUALLY. WE ARE UNSTUCK!

DAY 333
DAY 334

DAY 335

"The soul should always stand ajar, ready to welcome the ecstatic experience."

Emily Dickinson

DAY 337

DAY 338
You're transported into now.
Surprise catapults you into acute awareness. You forget the past (this is happy oblivion) and don't expect the future. This is that elusive "now" everyone talks about.

"Visual surprise is natural in the Caribbean: it comes with the landscape, and laced with its beauty, the sigh of History dissolves."

— Derek Walcott

DAY 339

DAY 340

Moved to... where?
THERE'S NO PREDICTING WHERE A SURPRISE WILL MOVE US, BUT ONE THING IS LIKELY: it will shift us out of any static focus on ourselves.

DAY 343

Margaret Mead...

"NEVER FORGET THAT YOU ARE A UNIQUE INDIVIDUAL, JUST LIKE EVERYONE ELSE."

DAY 344

DAY 345
DAY 346

"*Love means to learn to look at yourself the way one looks at distant things for you are only one thing among many. And whoever sees that way heals his heart, without knowing it, from various ills – A bird and a tree say to him: **Friend.***"

CZESLAW MILOSZ, FROM THE POEM "LOVE"

DAY 347 & DAY 348

A-MAZE-MENT

Surprise plunges you into the unknown. You feel lost, disoriented—it is truly "amazing." Where there was the familiar, there is space. It feels like wonder. So it is that surprise not only gets you lost but steers your way.

DAY 349 & 350

DAY 351

"Wonder is involuntary praise."
— Edward Young

DAY 352

AMAZING GRACE

Amazing Grace, how sweet the sound,
That saved a wretch like me.
I once was lost but now am found,
Was blind, but now I see.

T'was Grace that taught my heart to fear.
And Grace, my fears relieved.
How precious did that Grace appear
The hour I first believed...

John Newton

Open enough to be transported out of a narrow self, *moved into the moment, lost in amazement.* This sounds like life the way our most beloved mystics have described it to us.

SPIRITNG
SURPRISE

DAY 357

DAY 358:

"I AM AWAKE."
BUDDHA

DAY 359

DAY 360

DAY 361

"I am the spirit of the morning sea, I am the awakening and the glad surprise." RICHARD WATSON GILDER

DAY 364

DAY 362

DAY 363

"Our brightest blazes of gladness are commonly kindled by unexpected sparks."

Samuel Johnson

DAY 365

> "**Man's greatest achievement IS ASTONISHMENT.**"
> Johann Wolfgang von Goethe

Heartfelt thanks to:

John Addlesperger, for the most concrete of support; Diane Redman, for whom this book was first made as a birthday gift long ago (in part because I can always present her with my beginning offerings in any creative endeavor and receive whole-hearted appreciation); Jenae Neeson, a singularly talented and intuitive creative who is so fun to collaborate with; and Leah Campbell Badertscher and all my colleagues in her Art School classes for a most transformative, joyful, and, yes, *delightfully surprising year.*

www.ingramcontent.com/pod-product-compliance
Lightning Source LLC
Chambersburg PA
CBHW062026290426
44108CB00025B/2799